# Live with intention

Writing in a journal can be a powerful way to create a sacred space. It can be a mirror to your inner self, a place to explore, express, play, doodle, let your imagination dance, or just relax.

Sometimes you may see a clear purpose of intention. Other times, by reviewing what you've created in your journal, your intentions may emerge, your dreams may be revealed, and your memories may be opened.

You are invited to discover, experiment, enjoy...

Renée Locks
Mill Valley, California

Renée Locks is an artist, writer, calligrapher and poet, who expresses her love of nature through the delicate strokes and swirls of her sumi brush.

This collection of powerful words and images allows us to slow down and focus inward so that we may hear our greater calling.

We
do not
remember
DAYS;
We
remember
moments.

Just
Trust
yourself.

Then
you
will
know
how
To
Live.

.GOETHE

I dwell
in
possibility

EMILY
DICKINSON

you will do
foolish
things
but do them
with
ENTHUSIASM

/COLETTE

Life
is too
short
to
wear
tight
shoes

...and then
the day came
when the risk
to remain tight
in a bud was
more painful
than the risk
it took to
blossom.

— ANAIS NIN

Life is either
A Daring
adventure
or
nothing.

HELEN KELLER

whatever
you can do,
  or dream
you can do,
  you can.
Boldness.
  has a genius,
magic
    and power
  To it.

- G O E T H E

The challenge
is to be
yourself
in a
world
that is
trying
to
make
you
like
everyone
else

may your
life
be like a
wildflower
growing
freely
in the beauty
and joy
of each day

- INDIAN PROVERB

Be patient
dear heart.
Life's plans
like lilies,
pure and
white,
unfold.

We find
our way
one
step
at
a time.

show me
the person
who
never
makes a mistake
and I'll show
you the
person
who
never
makes
anything.

—UNKNOWN

Invest
in your
NOW

when
one door
closes,
another
one
opens...
somewhere

Right now
my life is
just ONE
Learning
Experience
after
another.

By the
end of
The
week
I
should
be A
Genius.

- JEANETTE OSIAS

Luck is
being
prepared
for

Opportunity
when it
comes.

— CITY OF HOPE

If you think
you're too
small
to be
effective
you
have never
been in bed
with a
mosquito.

BETTE REESE

A diamond
is a chunk
of coal
that made
good under
pressure.

Angels can fly
because
they take themselves
lightly

When your HEART Speaks, Take good NOTES.

ANDY MELLON

You cannot do
a kindness
too soon
because you
never know
how soon
will be
too late.
RALPH WALDO
EMERSON

Take
A
Little
Quiet
Time
Every
Day

Remember:
To remember
the sweet things
that happen
to you.

I have
decided
To be
happy
because
its good
for one's
health.

ITS OKAY TO WAKE UP
LAUGHING.

The future belongs
To those
who believe
in the BEAUTY
of their
Dreams.

Love comforts
like
Sunshine
After rain.

Let us
live the
Highest
Vision
of
what is
possible

INGA
GRACE

Live with intention.

Walk to the edge.

Listen hard.

Practice wellness.

Play with abandon.

Laugh.

Choose with no regret.

Continue to learn.

Appreciate your friends.

Do what you love.

Live as if this is all there is.

– mary anne radmacher

## Brush Dance